MY LITTLE TOWN

TOWN

BRIAN J. SMITH

AuthorHouse™
1663 Liberty Drive
Bloomington, IN 47403
www.authorhouse.com
Phone: 1 (800) 839-8640

Published by AuthorHouse 04/07/2015

ISBN: 978-1-5049-0574-9 (sc)
ISBN: 978-1-5049-0575-6 (e)

Library of Congress Control Number: 2015905247

Print information available on the last page.

Any people depicted in stock imagery provided by Thinkstock are models,
and such images are being used for illustrative purposes only.
Certain stock imagery © Thinkstock.

This book is printed on acid-free paper.

authorHOUSE®

__Preface__

There is a town in north Ontario
With dream comfort memory to spare

All my changes were there.

Neil Young, from his song *"Helpless"*, 1970

Whenever anyone asks me where I'm from, I don't hesitate to say, "Ingersoll"! Ingersoll is my hometown, yet I only lived there for a few years of my impressionable youth. Even though I left Ingersoll a long time ago and made my home in other cities, my heart often returns to the town I call home.

There are a few reasons for writing this book. First, I wanted to write a sequel to the international blockbuster "My Year On the Farm". I have a passion for history, but the stories of my ancestors from County Kilkenny in Ireland and Croydon, England were never written down, leaving me with a yearning to know something about my predecessors. I want to put pen to paper and create a record of my youth so I can pass it on to my grandchildren and future generations.

My mother is presently in the early stages of dementia. I ask her questions about the past and she cannot recollect details of the past with any clarity. Her memories are lost in a murky, confusing fog. If the same fate happens to me, my memories of the past will also disappear in twenty-five years. It is important to document and bear witness to an earlier time while I still have the clear ability to remember.

When I began writing, I found certain themes emerging. Music has always been vital to my life. The soundtrack of my adolescence in the late 1960's and early 1970's has left me with such bias towards that golden age of popular song that all other eras of music have lost their lustre. Education became a significant theme as I recalled the crucial influence my schools and teachers had on me since I chose to follow in their footsteps as an educator. Religion became a focus of the book as I recalled the powerful foundation various churches provided for me. Friends are so important to anyone growing up, and I was very fortunate to have wonderful compassionate friends to share the exuberance of my youth. Everyone remembers their first jobs, and my early employment in Ingersoll was an interesting learning experience.

I have chosen to include mostly pleasant stories in the recounting of my younger days since I didn't really face any serious personal challenges at the time. There was some stress in the family as there is in all families, but the desire to "put on a brave face" and "keep up appearances" was compelling because we were in a community where you knew nearly everyone and the humiliation of scandal is magnified in a small town. There is some balance to the stories since I included some schooling anxieties, ordeals with friends and the distress of some employment experiences.

As Neil Young put it, "dream, comfort memory to spare" pretty much sums up my feelings about Ingersoll. "And in my mind, I still need a place to go". That place is Ingersoll.

Dedicated to my wife Sherry, who I met in Ingersoll

IN MY LITTLE TOWN

TO THINK THAT ONLY YESTERDAY...

When I was 12 years old, I practiced a piece of music entitled *"Forgotten Dreams"* by Leroy Anderson. Nice little soft-chord piano song. What intrigued me most about the piece was the title; *Forgotten Dreams*. Dreams that are lost to the sands of time. I suppose it would be OK to forget dreams about being swallowed by an alligator, but what about bigger Dreams with a capitol D? What about the childhood dreams you have about your life? About the kind of person you might become, what kind of career you might have, who you might marry, where you might live?

As I was growing up, I had a Life dream about my hometown, Ingersoll. I would finish high school, go to university and train to be a music teacher, and graduate just in time to return to Ingersoll and replace the retiring music teacher, Mr. Riddolls. I would probably live in one of those nice big houses at the top of Oxford Street. I would keep a strong connection to the various churches I performed at. I would teach an entire generation of young students a variety of musical instruments and gain the respect of the community as the devoted high school music teacher, like my mentor, Harold Riddolls.

This was a strong dream about living the rest of my days in Ingersoll and kept me motivated in my studies throughout my university years. However, it never came to pass. When I graduated, the music job at the high school was taken by someone who could actually play stringed instruments. My specialty was brass instruments. When the offer of a career to teach music in Kitchener came up, I wisely took it. The dream of spending my life in Ingersoll was over. In time, the young dream has almost been forgotten.

I WAS CHEERFUL, BRIGHT AND...

If you were to walk through downtown Ingersoll with my father in the early 1970's, you would feel like there was a political campaign going on. Waves to the left and right, handshakes, nods to passersby and acquaintances, greetings all around. However, there was no political campaign, this was just a typical day in a town where you literally knew everybody.

I recall sitting up on the back seat of a brand new 1968 Chevy Camero convertible driven by our landlord Dan Dunlop with other neighbours as we drove through town to his Fleischer and Jewett car dealership. Blaring from the car radio was the tune "For What It's Worth" by Buffalo Springfield. Waving to classmates as we cruised the main street. This memory captures the excitement of the late 1960's and the place I have always called my "hometown".

Downtown Ingersoll

INGERSOLL

Ingersoll was the third largest town in Oxford County following Woodstock and Tillsonburg. For twenty years from 1950 to 1970, the population of 8,000 citizens remained unchanged. Situated on the Thames River on the main rail line, Ingersoll was a commercial center and factory town where cheese and milk were processed. My grandfather and father once worked at the Borden Milk factory. My aunts worked at Checkerboard Farms processing turkeys. Across from my school was the Ingersoll Casket Company where the whirring blades of band saws split the silence of a math test. The Catholic School kids had to put up with the constant clanging of the Morrow Screw and Nut factory right across their school on Thames street.

My roots in Ingersoll go back many generations on my mother's side. The Thomases and Heeneys farmed the land South of town in the 1800's. My paternal grandfather, Fred Smith, emigrated to Ingersoll from England right after World War One and took up a new trade as an electrician. Uncle Terry was valedictorian of IDCI's Class of 1948. I went to school with many cousins. Dad lived all but 16 of his 81 years in the town. There was a strong sense of belonging to Ingersoll.

Ingersoll was famous for the "Big Cheese". There was a plaque on the drive into town to commemorate this distinction. Back in 1866, dairy producers in the area cooperated to produce a 7,300 pound block of cheese to promote the local cheese industry. This mammoth hunk of fromage was shipped to New York State Fair and then on to London, England. Nothing on the plaque details what the slab of cheese smelled like when it arrived in London, but it was obviously a big deal at the time of Canada's Confederation. Nothing else for the next hundred years distinguished Ingersoll as much as a three-ton chunk of cheese.

In keeping with the spirit of promoting the cheese heritage of Ingersoll, there was a weeklong celebration of civic pride known as the Ingersoll Cheese and Wine Festival. Not much cheese was manufactured in town at the time, and no wine was produced, but citizens needed some excuse to party. Many events such as a parade, grape stomp, beauty contest, auto show, talent show and of course cheese and wine tasting transpired during this fall fair held every September. These events were very well attended at the time of my childhood in Ingersoll. I particularly liked the "curd cart" in the middle of town where you could purchase a small bag of cheese curds for twenty-five cents during the festival.

OUR HOUSE WAS A VERY, VERY, VERY FINE HOUSE...

Arriving from the farm in the summer of 1967, we rented 226 Oxford Street for 16 months then moved to 127 Ann Street by Christmas, 1968. The home had been relatively unchanged since it was built in the 1920's, but we soon made some improvements such as a new kitchen and stone fireplace. It was spacious and roomy with three bedrooms upstairs, good sized living room, dining room, den and kitchen on the main floor with a partially finished basement. A very large maple tree dominated the back yard followed by a long narrow stretch of lawn which was ideal for football practice. I was pretty much in charge of cutting the lawn on this property throughout the 1970's.

Neighbours included the unmarried elderly Capstick ladies next door. Occasionally we would find one of them staring from her window into our house. John Loveridge and his family lived on the other side in their large, stately red-brick home with extensive gardens in the back. Just two doors down were the Fleischers who had children the same age as our family. I used to hang out with Mark and my sister played with Cathy Fleischer. Ted Fleischer was co-owner of Fleischer and Jewett car dealership and he was known to arrive home and begin gardening in his backyard before he changed out of his suit and tie. Janet Fleischer was a wonderful caring woman who I got to know better when I worked at the Ingersoll Times newspaper where I was a reporter and she was a typesetter.

Backyard of 127 Ann St. Ingersoll

127 Ann Street, Ingersoll

WE ARE FAMILY

"Hey, do you think this brown patterned tie goes with my blue plaid pants?" Better ask Phil because he found a way to combine striped grey pants with a striped shirt, patterned suit jacket and swirling gold tie. Yes, it was the early 1970's when everybody got very creative with fashion. In the autumn of 1971 our family posed for what is one of our only portraits. Our neighbour, Phil Fleischer had taken up photography as a hobby and he set up his lights and camera in our living room while we looked around in our closets for our best clothes. The results speak for themselves.

My father, Jack, worked in Woodstock at the Firestone tire assembly plant as a factory electrician. He got involved in a lot of community activities such as Superintendant of Sunday school, Chair of Public Utilities Commission, Minor hockey coaching and sports writer for the local newspaper. My mother, Noreen was a registered nurse and was employed at the local Alexandra Hospital. Later in the 1970's Noreen would take a variety of university night courses eventually earning a Bachelor of Arts at the University of Western Ontario. Both shared a common interest in social work through a community based help-line called Telecare. They had a wide circle of friends including the Martins, Ranneys, Hills, and Griffins.

Me on left with mother Noreen, father Jack sister Brenda and brother Phil

6

Our household tried to have regular family meals with everyone in attendance, yet with mom's shift work and school activities it became increasingly difficult. Dad often cooked a roast beef dinner on Sundays and was quite successful as a chef. Occasionally we served a cow's tongue which seemed perfectly normal to our family but tended to gross out visitors. One interesting meal that mom attempted a few times was "cabbage rolls". I think the idea was to have fully-cooked rice embedded into fully-cooked ground beef, roll each beef patty into a cabbage and cover the delicacy with tomato soup. Bake for one hour. Unfortunately, in the haste to get the food on the table, we often ended up with kernels of partially cooked rice stuck to partially cooked beef in a concoction that was half-baked. Eventually when I heard we were having cabbage rolls for supper, I looked around for something else to eat.

My brother Phil was very interested in sports, especially basketball and football, becoming a very valuable player on all the teams he participated in. His large set of friends were often members of his sports teams. Sister Brenda also had many friends, and has kept in contact with several of them over the years. Brenda and I shared many experiences on our family vacations such as Florida in 1970 and especially Uncle Terry's Cottage. There are stories I could tell about my parents and siblings, but think it wise to concentrate on my own stories and save their stories for another book.

THE TIMES THEY ARE A-CHANGING

Soon after arriving in Ingersoll in 1967, I took on an after-school activity of delivering newspapers to the townspeople. The daily newspaper was the Toronto Star and I had about 15 regular customers scattered throughout the south side of town. This job provided me with adequate pocket money spent mostly on candy and weekly movies.

Trudging through the town every day with a heavy sack of papers in all kinds of weather also provided a great source of exercise. I also found myself reading the headlines and stories as I unpacked the newspapers outside Boniface's Variety store on the corner of Thames and King.

The events of 1968 proved to be of great historical consequence. The Vietnam War cast a long shadow over all events at the time, the way incidents in the Middle East dominate the news cycle today. Martin Luther King Jr. was assassinated on April 4 and America erupted into a week of race riots. Robert Kennedy seemed destined to become president but was also gunned down two months later. The hopes and dreams of an entire generation seemed shattered. Then, Trudeaumania swept the country as politics became much more exciting in Canada. The cold war raged on as Soviet tanks crushed the uprising in Czechoslovakia. Two American black athletes raised their fists in protest at the XIX Olympiad in Mexico City. After that, Richard Nixon won a close election to become President of the United States. Finally, at Christmas, the Apollo 8 astronauts sent back the incredible first pictures of planet Earth from the dark side of the moon.

These events had a lasting impact on me. It seemed that one crazy thing after another happened each day that I unwrapped the newspapers for delivery. I found myself identifying with the anti-war protesters and pop musicians of the day. I became one of the first of my grade eight class to wear my hair longer and stopped going to Paul the Barber who only knew buzz-cuts. At one point I got my grandma Isabelle to cut my hair by putting a bowl over my head. It was rather unique for a child of

12 to grow their hair long in Ingersoll in 1968, but by the early 1970's it seemed that all young boys were growing their hair long. Anyway, the shock of the 1964 Beatles long hair had long passed and by the time of the Abby Road album (1969), George Harrison had hair almost to his waist.

I also developed an allegiance towards left-wing politics. . For years in the upstairs washroom, a copy of the book, "Triumph and Tragedy: the Story of the Kennedys" provided interesting reading. I must have read through that book about 50 times. I was fascinated by Pierre Elliot Trudeau as he seemed to be portrayed as a dashing figure in full technicolor while all other politicians were in drab black and white. My parents also greatly influenced my political viewpoint as they both eagerly supported the Liberal cause. At election time, they always got a red Liberal sign posted on the front lawn to declare to the whole town our allegiance to Trudeau. Trudeau became the only Prime Minister I ever knew for all the days I lived in Ingersoll, except for 200 days of Joe Clark's government in 1979.

The leaves are a-changing on West Oxford road.

I GREW UP BELIEVING...

ST. JAMES ANGLICAN

Sundays always meant going to Church. From the time I arrived in Ingersoll in 1966 until I left for Kitchener in 1980, I had a strong connection with various churches in town. The most significant throughout my Ingersoll years was St. James Anglican church. Cub Scouts held all of their activities in the catacombs of the basement. Phys. Ed. class meant running around in the unkempt gymnasium below the Parish Hall. Over 60 children regularly filled the Hall every week for Sunday school classes. When you reached the end of Sunday School, there was confirmation class held in a special upstairs room directed by the minister's wife, Mrs. Sadler. During my grade eight year, there was also an exclusive after-school confirmation class conducted by the minister himself, Reverend Sadler. I recall having to memorize the Nicene Creed and asking the minister to explain how the creed says Jesus was "begotten, not made" and what was the difference?

St. James Anglican Church, Ingersoll

After I was confirmed into the Anglican Church, I enlisted in the Altar Boy Guild. Most of my duties required getting to church for the weekly Sunday 8:30 a.m. Communion Service. Arriving sleepy eyed, I would button up the long red cossock, then pull over the white surplice, then the large cross necklace and in seconds I would be transformed into an angelic altar boy. I would hoist the long pole cross right after entering the lush red carpeted interior of the church and service would begin. It was often just Reverend Sadler conducting the service for about 20 regular parishioners with me assisting. We would all turn to page 67 of the Book of Common Prayer and follow it line by line every single Sunday as the service never changed. I particularly remember reciting; "We do not presume to come to this thy Table, O merciful Lord, Trusting in our own righteousness, But in thy manifold and great mercies. We are not worthy so much as to gather up the crumbs under Thy Table..." Very serious, humbling words indeed, but so rich in Shakespearean eloquence.

Confirmation class 1971. I am third from left, Rev. Sadler is fifth from right

My main duties would commence when Reverend Sadler prepared the bread and wine for the communion sacraments. I would hand him the wine, then the holy water and he would mix the two and then acquire the necessary amount of small white wafers that signified bread. People would walk up to the altar and kneel as the reverend would place the small wafer in their hand, then he would place the chalice to their lips for a small drink of wine. If the minister over-estimated how much wine was needed for the service, he had to drink it all at the end of the service in one big gulp.

For all of my high-school years, I was a member of the Altar Guild and assisted with regular Sunday services, particularly the early 8:30 a.m. service. In my last year as altar boy, Reverend Sadler retired and Reverend Tom Griffin became minister. "Father Tom" brought a friendlier, lighter touch to the proceedings, but after a few months of serving Rev. Griffin, I was off to university and my career as altar boy ended.

When not needed as an altar boy, I often joined the choir as I had a keen interest in music. Eventually, I attained enough competence on the church organ to play for special services. I recall the first service I performed all by myself was a 7:30 a.m. Easter sunrise service in 1973 when I was 16 years old. It was exhilarating to pull out all the stops and play the rousing hymn "Jesus Christ is Risen Today" at the conclusion of the service. Every summer for the next six years, I played the organ for the Anglican weekly services.

GOD KEEPS HIS EYE ON US ALL...

My connection with the United Church on King Street came when I joined "Tyros" - a weekly club for young kids, something like Cub Scouts. I had a lot of fun playing floor hockey and making a tie holder craft for my father. In the Spring of 1968, I went on a weekend camp retreat with all the other United Church kids. Later during my university years, I was the organist at this large church for a few weddings.

The Catholic Church at the corner of Belmont and Thames became familiar to me when I joined the "folk group" and we performed every month. The white marble walls and flooring made it very "live" acoustically as the sound of our instruments echoed loudly through the cathedral. The Catholic church mass was very familiar as it followed closely the order of the Anglican service. I recall being at an evening mass when Bishop Emmett Carter, Bishop of London gave a rather angry sermon. "Where do you think priests come from?" he thundered to the congregation. He was admonishing the parishioners for not sending any Ingersoll residents to seminary to become priests. I had never heard anything like it before; a minister basically shouting and yelling to the congregation.

The final house of worship where I had a strong connection was the Presbyterian Church on Thames Street. I was hired for a year as church organist for the year I attended Teacher's College. Everyone in the small choir was very supportive of my efforts. Soon after I arrived, the church purchased a large expensive piano and I performed weekly Preludes on the piano before directing the hymns and anthems from the old pipe organ. It was a great chance to put all my training in music education to practical use. However, by April 1980 I received a job offer for a teaching position in Kitchener and my tenure as church organist and choirmaster was over.

Sacred Heart Catholic Church

St. Paul's Presbyterian Church

THEY'RE GONNA PUT ME
IN THE MOVIES...

A favourite cultural activity was going to the movies on weekends. The Strand theatre screened first-run movies and often presented "double features" where two movies were shown back-to-back. I would take my 50 cent allowance down to the theatre where admission price was only 35 cents for children 12 and under and I could buy a soft drink for the remaining 15 cents. I would try to mooch off some other kid's popcorn. The movies would end around 11 o'clock and I would walk home alone feeling rather safe in the small town.

Some of the top movie stars of the late 1960's such as John Wayne and Henry Fonda were well known from my dad's childhood in the 1930's. I recall my father and I particularly enjoyed Jimmy Stewart as the patriarch in a civil war saga called "Shenandoah". However, I found my real passion to be Clint Eastwood's western movies; *Fistfull of Dollars, The Good, the Bad and the Ugly* and *Hang 'Em High*.

Chomping on a cigarillo and hiding his guns or dynamite under his poncho, Clint was electrifying as the lone unsung hero. The music themes provided by Ennio Morricone also left a lasting impression on me.

Another very notable movie at the time was *"2001: A Space Odyssey"*. The thrilling soundtrack from Richard Strauss written 60 years earlier really caught the exhilaration of space travel with its upward spiralling symphonic sound. The cascading light show as the astronaut travelled through space was a trip to behold! The obstinate computer with a mind of its own portends some current issues regarding artificial intelligence. At a time when men were getting ready to walk on the moon, the suggestion that manned Mars missions would be routine by 2001 was perfectly plausible to me in 1968. Maybe in my lifetime it may happen.

The Strand theatre didn't seem to care what age you were to see any kind of movie. I just showed up at the theatre, paid my admission and sat down. One time there was this movie entitled *"Barbarella"* starring a young Jane Fonda. Well, the first thing that happens in the movie is a strip tease out of her astro suit while floating through space. Later in the movie she gets trapped into something called an "orgasmatron". I was eleven years old at the time and was not prepared for such adult fare. However, I'm pretty sure I left the theatre that night with a smile on my face.

Ingersoll's cinema closed down for good in the early 1970's. Perhaps the competition from nearby Woodstock and London led to its demise. The inauguration of cable television was probably another factor in the passing of the Strand theatre. All of a sudden we could get 12 television stations instead of just two. Anyway, the town's movie theatre was a great pastime when I was a kid and an important part of my childhood. Eventually the cinema was converted into the Ingersoll Theatre for the Performing Arts where live action plays are performed. This is indeed a wonderful transition for the theatre of my youth.

LISTEN TO THE MUSIC...

One thing I am eternally grateful for was my parents continued support of my piano music lessons. I had developed a good rapport with my private teacher Mrs. Ranney in Salford and continued for eight consecutive years. My parents were always available to drive me out to Salford every week for my lessons. Although her music curriculum was mostly the grading of the Royal Conservatory of Music, she also provided helpful extra group classes in music rudiment theory. She was also rather innovative by encouraging piano duets at recitals. By the time I was in grade six public school, I was taking the Grade Six Royal Conservatory piano exams.

The first time I accompanied my father on piano was in the winter of 1968. The song was "Somewhere My Love" from the recent film, Dr. Zhivago. Dad was a self-taught musician with a wonderful, powerful voice, but he had a manner of singing songs his own way, despite what was clearly written by the composer. I recall getting into a slight disagreement with him about the line "Although the snow covers the hope of spring." He insisted on singing "All *through* the snow, covers the hope of spring." Didn't make much grammatical sense, but he performed it his way at a parent-teacher meeting at the school. For many years after, I accompanied dad at weddings and other church functions. I learned from him to let the soloist interpret the music whatever way they want and a good accompanist just *follows* the soloist without getting bogged down on pesky little details about what the composer wrote.

After strict adherence to the Royal Conservatory method of practicing scales and arpeggios and performing Bach and Beethoven, my interest started to turn towards playing pop songs. I noticed that nearly all popular music printed guitar chords above the staff, so I developed a method of just playing the melody with the right hand and improvising an accompaniment pattern based on guitar chords with my left hand. This really speeded up the process of playing through an entire book of popular music as I could quickly play with both hands nearly any pop song that I wanted.

However, there was an unfortunate consequence to leaving the foundation of a good classical music education at a young age in favour of impressing other kids with an ability to play a variety of pop songs. A hot house tomato grows quickly to impressive size but doesn't have much flavour. Too much icing tends to spoil a cake. There is such a thing as having too much style and not enough substance. Similarly, by the time I entered the Faculty of Music at the University of Western Ontario, I noticed that the best piano works of the great masters were beyond my grasp as I lacked the discipline to practice the fundamental scales, chords and arpeggios necessary for excellent performance. I now look back with some regret at the missed opportunities I had to really practice and develop my piano skills as a teenager. Laying around the house and watching "The Price Is Right" and other game shows through the summer was in retrospect a complete waste of time.

It is important to know how exceptionally brilliant the quality of popular music was at this time. In the Summer of '69 I would sit for hours listening to the radio tuned to 68.0 CHLO St. Thomas. They would play the top 40 songs and do a countdown to the number one song. It was an eclectic mix of rock, folk, country, gospel and blues when the Beatles and Rolling Stones were topping the charts. Creedence Clearwater Revival, the Guess Who, Simon and Garfunkel, and Gordon Lightfoot were a few of the great artists whose music played daily on the radio. In my high school years, I would also be greatly influenced by Elton John, Chicago, Blood, Sweat and Tears, James Taylor and Billy Joel. If I heard a piece that I liked, I would go downtown to Foster's Appliance Store and buy a 45 rpm single vinyl record of the song and hurry back home to play it over and over on my portable record player. Then I would go over to the piano and try to play whatever I could of the song by ear.

Sometimes the "B" side of a single was better than the "A" or featured side. For instance, I wasn't particularly fond of the Rolling Stones and favoured the Beatles. I thought Mick Jagger just strutted around and shouted instead of sang and the whole band sounded like it was out of tune most of the time. However, my schoolmate Kevin Sheppard was a big fan of the Stones and convinced me to purchase my only Rolling Stones 45; "Honky Tonk Woman". It was a reasonably good rousing tune with a trademark guitar riff from Keith Richards, but the big surprise came when I flipped the record over to hear the other side. The Rolling Stones released "You Can't Always Get What You Want" as the "B" side to "Honky Tonk Woman" and it is a far superior song. With meaningful lyrics and orchestral and choir accompaniments, this piece gave me a whole new respect for the quality of songs written by Mick Jagger and Keith Richards.

The best example of a "B" side greatly surpassing an "A" side was when I purchased "I'm Free" by the Who. This was a catchy single that clocked in at 1:58 or slightly less than two minutes. However, when you flipped the record over to the "B" side, you got three great songs played consecutively from their upcoming rock opera "Tommy". Nearly seven minutes of the best of the Who.

45 rpm single vinyl records. CD's of the 1960's.

PUT ME IN COACH, I'M READY TO PLAY...

My fondest memory of involvement in team sports was my participation in minor league baseball in the Spring of 1968. Our team had an excellent coach in Larry Bannon and I found myself really enjoying the competition and once hit a rare inside-the-park home run to the delight of teammates and spectators. The team was small enough that I was participating on the field all the time. However, the next year was a different story. I was in a team with many more players and found myself sitting on the bench through most of the games and never seemed to get a chance to prove myself to the coach. Eventually in the middle of the season I just stopped going to games and quit. This would mark the end of my participation in team sports for the rest of my life. Never again any formal league hockey, baseball, football or basketball.

Perhaps the summit of my sports career came at the end of grade eight. Victory Memorial School had a "field day" of athletic competition where I opted to compete in the 100-year dash. I didn't join any runners club or have any coaching, as the event was just a friendly competition among schoolmates. For me, there was no warming up, stretching of limbs, or strategy, it was just "run like hell" after the starters pistol. To my surprise, I beat all the boys in my class in the first race, then all the grade eight boys in the final. This qualified me for the inter-county championships in Woodstock held at College Avenue Secondary School. Soon after the bus pulled up, I was set to run in my qualifying heat. Unfortunately, there was much more stiff competition from the Woodstock boys. I came in dead last. My race was finished at about 9:20 a.m. and I had nothing to do for the rest of the day until the bus left for Ingersoll at 3:30. I recall wandering the streets and parks of Woodstock for a full day until it was time to go home.

As I write this in 2015, my mother Noreen is in a retirement home on Fife Ave. in Woodstock, right across from College Avenue Secondary School. There is a large window in the building that is directly across from the track and field of the school. It seems to be the only window where the elderly residents can witness everyday human activity. It was on that field that my sporting career reached its peak in 1970.

I came close to being involved in high school football. The coach, Mr. Cramp, knew of my brother's excellent athletic skills and invited me to try out for the school team. I lasted one day. He had me run up and down this steep hill about 10 times and I went bumping up against other boys in drill scrimmages. This experience at football practice wasn't any fun at all and I don't recall even throwing or catching a ball. I think he needed someone for defence. Anyway, I decided to drop out after one practice as I knew this kind of athletic team sport activity was not for me.

I much preferred riding my bike around the town and countryside as a form of exercise. A great way to spend a hot summer afternoon was to bike the 15 km. out to Verchoyle gravel pits, swim around for an hour, then bike home. I also enjoyed biking East on King Street about five km. past Centerville to a creek near West Oxford Church. I would spend hours with friends wading through the stream to catch crayfish. Biking has stayed with me as my favourite form of exercise for the rest of my life. I also enjoy hauling a canoe over my head and hiking through the wilderness from lake to lake, but that's another story.

BACK IN SCHOOL AGAIN....

VICTORY MEMORIAL SCHOOL

Victory Memorial School was built in 1919 to commemorate the successful conquest by Canadian troops in World War I. The fancy cannons mounted at the front of the school dated from the Crimean War of the 1850's. The schoolyard at the back had two entrances marked "Boys" and "Girls" and during recess the grounds were completely segregated with boys on one side and girls on the other. I once asked a teacher on duty what would happen if a boy purposefully crossed to the girl's side. "Why, you would get a detention" was her reply.

When the recess bell rang, our class would line up in the back cloak room and march out in double file to the music of John Phillip Sousa blaring from the loudspeakers. Paunchy principal Alistar Murray would take up his position at the second floor window, munch on an apple and knock loudly on the glass pane if the behaviour of the boys during recess got too rambunctious. After recess, the teachers would get us to line up again with our designated classes and wait until silence prevailed across the schoolyard before we marched back to class.

I arrived at the school in September 1967. It was a cool, cloudy, drizzly kind of day. I didn't know anyone in the class. My teacher was Mr. Knight; the first male teacher I ever had. He was a good-looking competent teacher with dark hair and dark framed glasses. In the first few minutes after O Canada and a Bible scripture reading, Mr. Knight read out the attendance roll. He would ask Cathy McBeath if the pronunciation was McBeeth or Shakespearean McBeth. When he got to calling out "Brian Smith", I put my hand up...and so did another student! There were two Brian Smith's in one grade 6 class! What were we going to do? He asked me what my middle name was. I replied "John". Thankfully, the other student's middle name was "Richard". From that moment on, I was known as Brian J. and the other guy was Brian R. To this day, my signature is always Brian J. Smith so as not to be confused with any other Brian Smith.

Victory Memorial School: Girls to the left, Boys to the right

For physical education in winter, we walked across the road and used the gymnasium in the basement of the parish hall at St. James Anglican church. The construction of a new gymnasium for the school would be completed in the fall of 1968. On one snowy day, our class was marched over to the church, but we became boisterous and unmanageable. Lots of pushing, shoving and yakking with me at the back of the line. I did not hear Mr. Knight shout; "the next person to talk is going to get a detention"! Suddenly everyone became silent except for me. I just kept on talking. I recall looking up at Mr. Knight and the pained look on his face as he realized he would have to babysit me for a half hour after class.

There was no racial diversity in the entire school. Everyone at the time was Caucasian. However, there was considerable economic and intellectual diversity. Children of doctors, lawyers and factory owners sat side-by-side with children who wore the same clothes every day and rarely washed. One of my first friends when I arrived in Ingersoll was the son of a single mother who struggled to feed her three children. One Saturday I had lunch at his house and four of us kids shared a can of tomato soup. Later in the year I became good friends with the dentists' son and enjoyed playing in their sprawling house and backyard. His father was also a pilot and he took us for a flight over Ingersoll. A few years later I would spend a week at their family's wonderful Temagami cottage.

My grade 7 teacher was Miss Dennison. She was about five feet tall, weighed about 250 lbs. and had very short cropped dark hair. Yet, in spite of her appearance, she was a very competent teacher. One strong memory I have from this grade was a "play day" our class had at the very end of the year. She walked our class down Canterbury Street, then down Wellington Street to Victoria Park where we played a friendly game of baseball. She was a good sport, donning a brightly coloured baseball cap and even got in on the action smacking the ball right out of the park and running the bases.

This is me in grade five

This is me in grade seven

The other interesting thing about grade seven was the introduction of Industrial Arts or "Shop" class for boys and "Home economics" for girls. Once a week for an afternoon, we would go to the basement of VMS and learn about various tools and work the lathe to create a wooden bowl. The girls went to the other basement side and learned how to cook and sew. Our teacher was Mr. Paul Jagoe, who also doubled as our physical education teacher. From my recollection, it seemed like the industrial tools installed in the 1920's were the same machines we were using in the late 1960's. These classes were intended to prepare boys for work in the many factories in town and the girls for a more domestic setting.

Perhaps my most influential teacher at VMS was my grade eight teacher, Stuart Little. I had also known him as my Sunday school teacher at St. James Anglican church. Tall and lanky with a bit of unkempt facial hair, looking much like a lumberjack, he was the one teacher that showed the most compassion, understanding and kindness towards students. He had a passion for history and enjoyed telling stories about the Battle on the Plains for Abraham, the War of 1812, Lord Durham's report, Confederation, Sir John A. MacDonald and Louis Riel. His enthusiasm for tales from the past probably stoked my own lifelong fascination with history.

During the school year, Mr. Little was off sick and we had a substitute teacher for a week. An energetic, feisty old lady with her hair tied up tightly in a bun looked up from her glasses straight at me and asked; "are you Jack and Noreen's son?" It was the kind of question that could be embarrassing in front of a grade eight class, but I answered, "yes". Who was this person who knew my parents, but I had no idea who she was? It turned out to be Mildred Batten, a great aunt from the Heeney family tree. This was the Spring of 1970, and I came to find that Aunt Mildred was born in 1896. Therefore, this sprightly lady who ran our class with expert skill was 74 years old at the time. I would come to know her better over the years and interview her when I became a History teacher and discover that she was a teacher for nearly six decades. Her vigorous industriousness and keen intelligence right up to her death at age 98 has been a great source of inspiration for me as I contemplate what seniors are capable of.

Memorization was a key pedagogical strategy in those days as Mr. Little required that all of our class recite from memory Psalm 121; "*I lift up mine eyes unto the hills*". We also had itinerant preachers occasionally appear before us from the various Protestant denominations in town to teach Religion. Other itinerant teachers included the music teacher who struggled to get the class to sing or play the recorder, and the art teacher who encouraged us to form small sculptures out of asbestos or Plaster of Paris. I recall creating a work of art that was a cardboard peace sign painted black, then splattered with red paint to look like blood stains. The art teacher was intrigued by this as I'm sure all the anti-Vietnam War protests on the nightly news were gaining a hold on my subconscious.

I had a different teacher for English and he had a fixation for teaching us everything about grammar. Every class meant dissecting a sentence and identifying nouns, verbs, pronouns, adjectives, adverbs and conjunctions . Then subject and predicate. Then participles and gerunds. Ad nauseam. I could feel my brain cells crying out for a release from this agony. I stopped doing grammar homework and even avoided participating in class. My marks in English dropped significantly into the low 60's and this had crucial implications when I arrived at high school.

It was a time when you could fail a class and be kept back from graduating and repeat the year all over again, possibly with the same teacher. I recall two students in my grade 8 class who were repeating with Mr. Little. Both of them seemed to get along very well in our class and actively participated the second time around. The girl was nearly 16 years old and had boyfriends from the high school drive over to meet her at lunch. The boy surely had a learning disability of some kind and had great difficulty in comprehending the various topics we were taught. It was a time before Special Education teachers assisted students with accommodations or Social Workers helped sort out students with complex family lives. Students who failed two or more core classes in a year had to repeat the entire grade the next year.

In the summer between grade eight and grade nine, I walked most days down to the Maude Wilson Memorial Pool for a swim. An elderly man named Buck Billings gave swimming lessons and you could hear his big booming voice yell; "Hold it...hold it...hold it...Blow!" Sometimes the pool was so crowded with kids in the shallow end you had to squeeze yourself into the water wherever you could. I recall line-ups for the diving board where I worked up the courage to dive head first. I jumped off the three meter board a few times but never had the nerve to dive head first from that height. The very busy pool put a strain on the archaic chlorination system as the pool water became increasingly cloudy as the summer wore on. Eventually the lifeguards blew a whistle at 20 minute intervals ordering everyone out of the pool so they could peer into the murky water to see if anyone had drowned. When no bodies were found, a whistle would blow and over a hundred kids would jump back into the pool.

Enjoying a cool swim in the pool.

DON'T KNOW MUCH ABOUT SCIENCE BOOKS...

INGERSOLL DISTRICT COLLEGIATE INSTITUTE

Ingersoll District Collegiate Institute (IDCI) was a sprawling campus of over 1,500 students. The main buildings of the high school were built in the 1950's and a new library/commercial/science/drama wing was constructed during my first year. Half the students were from the town and half came from the country. At the end of the day many buses would line up and take all the rural students home. This was indeed a different experience from my days at Victory Memorial School that enrolled perhaps 400 students.

Transitioning to high school is a somewhat traumatic experience for any youth. You go from being the top dog as a grade eight student lording your esteemed position over all other kids on the schoolyard to being the lowest runt of the litter in grade nine. To me, the graduating class of senior students seemed like mature adult men and women. **Initiation Day** was a tradition that let you know your humble place in the student hierarchy. I recall wearing an onion around my neck all day. My brother Phil brought a few heavy textbooks home just so I could carry them to school for him. In between classes, the seniors would make you walk backwards to each class. Generally some mildly humiliating things that older students imposed on the new scholars. This tradition ended when I became a senior student as we were instructed by the administration of the school to discontinue the long tradition of humiliating the incoming grade nine students. I had mixed feelings about the prohibition of Initiation Day as it was generally done in the spirit of good fun, yet there was evidence that some natural bullies carried things a bit too far. Yes, a few bad apples really do spoil the whole bunch.

One of the big surprises of grade nine came in my English class. I was given a series of booklets to read and write out responses to comprehension questions. I worked my way through the tasks and found myself far ahead of the rest of the students in the quantity and quality of assignments that I completed. The voluptuous Ms. Vardon was my teacher and she explained to me in mid-October that I was in the four-year college applied stream, yet I was showing potential for the five-year university academic stream. This was indeed surprising! I had ambitions of going to university, but you don't go to university unless you are taking academic English. It later dawned on me that my grade eight English teacher had placed me into the college stream because of my reluctance to complete all that grammar homework. No hauling me aside and telling me to pull myself up by my bootstraps if I had dreams of university. Just secretly placing me in the college stream with absolutely no consultation with me or my parents. Teachers back then had considerable power to decide unilaterally where students were placed. Thankfully, the IDCI administration through Ms. Vardon recognized that I belonged in the five-year stream and changed my classes around so that I was in an academic class after Christmas. By grade 12, English was one of my favourite classes with the lovely Ms. Duncan.

The greatest academic challenge for me in grade nine was Math class. Somewhere along the way I lacked the intellectual capacity to understand the transition from the manipulation of concrete numbers; 9(6-4)(3+1)= to abstract expressions; x(y-z)(a+b)=. There was a lot of yelling from the teacher, but my marks were sinking fast and I was failing math by the middle of the year. Thankfully, in March, I was given a two week opportunity to work one-on-one with a young student teacher from Althouse Teacher's College where he found out where my gap in comprehension was and gradually enhanced my understanding of mathematical concepts until I eventually caught up with the rest of the class.

The next year, in grade 10, I found myself sitting at an obtuse angle behind a very pretty girl. I would admire the way her derriere was positioned in the desk and contemplate whether her bottom shape was indeed spherical or conical. Breaking my daydream reverie was an old woman's scratchy voice commanding; "Brian! come to the board and find the asymptote!" Refraining from answering that I think I had already found the ideal assim-whatever, I sheepishly skulked to the front blackboard. After a couple of minutes of complete humiliation in front of the class where I demonstrated beyond any doubt that I had no idea what an asymptote was, I shuffled back to my seat. At that moment I vowed that I would immediately focus in class and complete all math homework to avoid the shame and embarrassment of looking like a complete dufus in front of my peers.

The old woman that called me to the blackboard was Mrs. Ackert. Everyone called her "Granny" Ackert. She was a short, serious lady who carried a yardstick in her hand and kept a very stern tone throughout every class. Her favourite pedagogical method was to call a student up to the blackboard and show the scholars how to do a math question. This method of trying to avoid disgrace worked very well for me. I had Granny Ackert for two years and gradually improved my Math performance until I was prepared for Calculus, Functions and applications in Physics in my senior years. I will forever be thankful that I had an excellent teacher like Mrs. Ackert. Sometimes the best teachers that you can ever have are the ones that challenge you.

French class was a disaster. First of all, the very first time I spoke a word of French was when I was thirteen years old in grade nine. This is far too late to begin a second language. Secondly, the very first lesson in the textbook instructed you to shout "Garcon!" if you wanted to get the attention of a waiter in a French restaurant. I tried this once on the Champs - Elysee and the fastidious waiter was indeed not amused. Lastly, the teacher took to wearing mini skirts and sitting on the front desk facing the class. After two years, I couldn't take it anymore and elected to take Latin - a much more useful language.

This is me in Grade nine   **This is me in Grade 11**

One of the optional subjects I took in high school was called Data Processing. There was this general buzz at the time that computers would one day be very important in the future. So I took this course where I was taught basic programming and filled out stacks of cards with penciled squares. We would bundle up the cards and send them off to the "computer" in London, Ontario. There was once a field trip to Althouse College to see the computer that took up an entire classroom. Lots of heavy duty steel, blinking lights and whirling tape reels from floor to ceiling. There was no such thing as a computer in Ingersoll at that time. Two weeks later a long sheet of paper would be distributed to the class showing the results of your programming. If there were no mistakes in the penciled cards and all cards remained in order, you got the desired result. Otherwise, you had to redo the programming and wait another two weeks to see your results. Today I have five personal computers in my household. We have come a very long way in computer technology since the early 1970's.

Perhaps the most rewarding experience for me at high school was my participation in the Musical production each year. These performances were a collaboration between the Drama and Music Departments and involved over a hundred students in such roles as make-up, costuming, set design and construction, back stage direction, musicians, dance and vocal chorus, and stage actors. I was always in the orchestra pit playing trombone. Even though it was a small contribution, I felt like I was associated with a very large group effort in creating a wonderful creative event. Oliver was staged in 1972, Guys and Dolls in 1973, then South Pacific in 1975. Brilliant actors included Dave Talbot, Jamie Petit and Susan Lyndon. The present mayor of Ingersoll, Ted Comisky, had a superb singing voice and had a leading role in all of the musicals at the time. I was very proud to see my future wife, Sherry Ramrattan, in the leading role of Nellie in South Pacific. She did a fantastic job. I'm sure the director arranged some devious irony by casting Sherry and caking her brown skin with white make-up as she played the role of a racist character, Nellie.

Although I often had the dream of being a music teacher at the back of my mind throughout high school, I had an impulsive change of career direction in my final year at IDCI. I thought I might want to become a dentist! I had known the dentist's son very well in my elementary school days and knew the affluence that a career like that could bring. So I dropped History and Arts courses and loaded my timetable with Biology, Chemistry, Physics, Calculus and Functions Math. There was hardly any room for Music in this timetable! However, after a few months immersed in Maths and Sciences, I eventually knew for certain that continuing in this track would be foolish as all that rational thinking did not align with my passion for the Arts. Therefore, I eventually decided to apply to the Faculty of Music at the University of Western Ontario and leave all that Science behind.

During that final year of high school I was very fortunate to be dating Sherry. She and I shared all of our classes together except music. She even joined the band and played saxophone. Since we had all those Math, Science and Latin classes together, we did our homework together and prepared for tests. Most of my memories of grade 13 were driving out to Salford manse nearly every school night to Sherry's house. We would spread the heavy Chemistry and Calculus textbooks over her dining room table and get all the necessary homework completed for the next day. What a wonderful study partner she was for those very challenging courses.

When we weren't studying together, Sherry and I enjoyed swimming

By far the most influential educator in my high school career was the music teacher, Mr. Riddolls. We both shared a passion for music. He showed a lot of compassion and concern for kids and took a sincere interest in the musical development of his students. As the only music teacher, he ran many extra-curricular programs such as orchestra, band, marching band, glee club, brass quintet, and direction of the yearly Musical production. He was the person in charge of undertaking the music trip to Florida in 1974. I participated in all of the programs that he directed.

As an example of his kindness, he once took my friend and I to a day-long music conference in St. Catherines. We attended a brass clinic where a famous trumpeter, Sergio Mendez, explained proper breathing, embouchure and tonguing techniques. I had never heard a solo trumpeter play with such full, warm tone and effortlessly overcome the sound of an entire back-up band in performance. After the clinic, Mr. Riddolls and his wife took us to nearby Niagara Falls and paid for our dinner, then back to St. Catherines for the evening concert. This is an example of where a teacher could easily go to a weekend music conference on his own, but decided to include students to benefit from the experience.

Through his example, I eventually decided that I would follow in his footsteps and pursue a career as a high school music teacher. He helped me prepare for university auditions at the Faculty of Music and became a real mentor to my dreams. Once at University, I called on him to perform an organ part on a Gabrielli Canzona, while my brass quintet performed at St. James Church. He was the pianist at my wedding, playing the processional and backing up my father's singing of "Sunrise, Sunset". We kept in touch over the years and when he passed away in 2006, at the ripe old age of 89, I was devastated at the loss of a kindred spirit.

IDCI Orchestra circa 1974, under the direction of Mr. Harold Riddolls.

At the end of my years at IDCI, I applied for and received the Firestone Scholarship. This scholarship was open to four Canadian graduates across Canada who had a graduating average over 80%. Since my father worked as an electrician at Firestone Canada in Woodstock, I was eligible to receive a major grant each year that I attended university. $1,400 every year for four years paid for tuition and books and some of my rent for a whole year! I supplemented this scholarship with summer jobs and avoided any student loans for the entire time at university.

Receiving the Firestone Scholarship with my parents, Noreen and Jack. Green bowties were in fashion.

YOU'VE GOT A FRIEND

DAVID GILL

It is rather stressful to arrive at a new school at age 10 and not know anyone. Fortunately, I was able to make great friends with some of the kids at my school. One of the first was David Gill, who invited me to his grade 6 birthday party in the autumn of 1967. Soon after the party, I was over to his house to play quite often. His father was a retired minister and his mother was a very interesting, intelligent woman who spent her formative years growing up in India as a child of missionaries. One day, Mrs. Gill brought many exquisite Indian treasures to our class such as carved elephants and bronze engravings for the kids to see. She told stories about Hindu gods and deities and you could tell she really adored India. However, in the Spring of 1968, Mr. Edgar Gill was called to a United Church congregation in Port Stanley to continue as a minister. So David and I arranged an exchange over the next four summers where he would come to Ingersoll and stay with my family for a week and I would go to his town and be with his family for a week.

Port Stanley was a wonderful beach resort town where we could go jumping in the waves of Lake Erie every day. You could purchase fresh fish from the dockside. One summer we paddled up and down Kettle Creek and competed in a canoe race. He had two bikes, so we sometimes spent an afternoon exploring an off-road trail. Exhausted at the end of the day, we would gather around the minister's bed and be encouraged to say our prayers. David and I would keep our prayers as short as could be admissible, but Mrs. Gill had lengthy, articulate prayers where she would comment on the "exuberance" of youth. This activity of saying prayers at the end of the day had a calming effect on us as we often slept soundly until the next day's adventures.

"That's one small step for man, One giant ?#shleep for mankind". "What'd he say?.. What'd he say?"

It was July 20, 1969. Dave and I had been anticipating this moment all day. The Apollo 11 spacecraft had been orbiting the moon and sent astronauts Neil Armstrong and Buzz Aldrin to the surface of the moon in their Lunar Excursion Module. Then came the dramatic announcement that "The Eagle has Landed". We were glued to the television set in keen anticipation for their walk on the moon. When the spectacular minute finally arrived where Neil stepped on the moon and uttered the immortal phrase, "That's one small step for man, one giant leap for mankind", we didn't know just what he had said because of the poor hissing audio reception. Thankfully, a few minutes later, the news reporter cleared it up and we all thought that was such a nice thing for Neil to say before planting an American flag on the moon.

I was in Port Stanley when the amazing Man on the Moon event took place and shared the event with Dave and his family as we huddled around the television. During that summer I became quite passionate about all things related to the Apollo moon landing and began collecting bubblegum cards depicting astronauts with appropriate names like Buzz Aldrin and Gus Grissom. The event inspired some cool popular music such as "Spirit in the Sky" and "Rocket Man".

When David came to Ingersoll, he would re-connect with his old childhood buddies. One day, about seven of us boys biked two hours down Sweaburg Road out to Shelton's gravel pit for a swim, then biked all the way back. In the summer of 1970, I recall going with him to watch the Beatle's movie "Let it Be" and thought what a depressing movie it was! John and Yoko huddling in a corner, Paul bickering with George on camera, it was a real let-down from the excitement of "A Hard Day's Night" and "Help". Nevertheless, the roof-top concert at the end of the movie was very interesting.

In the summer of 1975, when I was graduating from high school, David got a job managing a small, seedy motel outside Gravenhurst in the Muskokas. For the weekend I spent with him, he was the only person managing the six-room motel. In the mornings, we would wash and change the sheets and tidy the rooms and then spend the rest of the day hanging out in the woods behind the place or in the town. That was the last year I ever saw David, but I will always savour the memory of a good friend who introduced me to his interesting parents and the wonderful resort town of Port Stanley.

JUDD KENNEDY

Another fine friend from elementary school days was Judd Kennedy. We hung out at school and shared a passion for a new craze of Hot Wheels, the miniature race cars that you could send down a rubber track. Judd's father was Dr. Charles (Chuck) Kennedy, a dentist in town. One morning, Judd's dad drove us to the London airport where he piloted a small Cessna airplane with just us two boys as passengers. We flew over Ingersoll and did some banks and turns on a glorious sunny day in June 1968. What a cool thing that was! I recall Dr. Kennedy commenting that anybody could operate an airplane for take-off because you just had to keep the craft straight and accelerate. The real challenge for pilots was landing the aircraft where unexpected wind gusts can make the whole procedure very precarious. Thankfully, he did a great job of landing the plane after a wonderful ride.

Snowmobiles were a relatively new invention in the late 1960's. The Kennedy's bought one and there was a wide-open field right across the road from their house on Harris Street. On a few wintry nights, Judd and I would take the snowmobile for exhilarating fast rides dashing through the snow.

Most of what I remember Judd and I doing when we got together was capturing small insects and tossing them into spider webs to watch the spider capture, kill, then envelope the helpless creature in the web. Once we spent an afternoon in the creek behind what is now Elmhurst Inn wading through the water capturing small minnows and crayfish. Another time we biked out to the Verchoyle gravel pit water hole and spent most of the time trying to capture a very elusive slippery frog. These are the things that fascinated young boys in the days before video games.

I was very fortunate to be able to spend a week with Judd and his family at their cottage on Lake Temagami. This was a beautiful district of North Ontario with many scenic lakes and bays. We spent most of our time boating around looking for ideal fishing spots and putting a line in the water and occasionally catching Pike fish. A very strong memory was seeing my "moon shadow" for the first time. Judd and I were standing near the end of their dock on a clear starry night with a full moon. The light from the moon was strong enough to cast a shadow of ourselves onto the dock. Whenever I hear the song "Moon Shadow" by Cat Stevens, I think of that time in the beautiful Temagami region.

Sometime in the summer of 1969, Dr. Kennedy suffered a heart attack and spent a few weeks recovering in the hospital. Judd and I went to visit him a few times. What I remember most was the fact he had a private room all to himself instead of sharing a hospital room with any other patient. He survived this attack and returned pretty much to normal, but a massive heart attack in 1977 killed him.

Judd and I had a kind of falling out in the spring of 1971 over cadets. Ingersoll District Collegiate Institute had a compulsory program at the time of making every grade nine student participate in an army drill corps exercise after school for a month. IDCI had enough army surplus uniforms to outfit the entire school. You either went to cadets and did the marching drill or you sat in detention hall. I reluctantly sulked off to army training with a very bad attitude indeed. To my surprise, Judd was one of the "officers" of my platoon! He had joined the extra elite after school officer training program and suddenly I had to follow his orders for drill! I recall shuffling my feet and being rather uncooperative whenever he gave us commands and generally making life difficult for Judd. After cadets ended, Judd and I went our separate ways.

I now feel really embarrassed regarding my lack of respect for Judd during cadets. His father played an important role in training pilots for World War II. Both my grandfathers served in World War I. He and his family had shown me generous kindness for the years we were friends. I had been strongly influenced by the anti-war movement and identified much more with long-haired hippies than buzz-cut army drill types. Anyway, forcing Ingersoll's young high-school students to join a military drill practice was abolished the next year as cadets became voluntary and pretty much died out by the time I graduated. Ironically, I joined the school Marching Band under the direction of Harold Riddolls and participated in the cadet program indirectly for the next few years anyway. Further irony occurred much later in my life when I became assistant director of the Ceremonial Band of the Waterloo Region Police Service. My grade nine marching training was a great advantage after all!

Judd did not return to IDCI for grade 10. He went off to private school and I hardly ever saw him again. What little I knew about private school I learned from the lawyer's son, John McBride. I was his golfing buddy in the summer of 1971 and he attended private school right after elementary school. I found out that tuition was very expensive; thousands of dollars that my parents could not afford. The other thing about private school was a compulsory study hall every night for two hours after dinner. Students were required to sit in a large room and do homework or study for tests or get extra help from teachers every single night. No wonder the doctors and lawyers of our society mostly come from private schools with all that extra academic training!

MARY LOU ROBOTHAM

Mary Lou was my first girlfriend. We were in the same classroom in grade six and grade eight and she was always one of the top students academically. I have always admired girls who are intelligent. We started walking home together after school and going to hockey games or the movies. Occasionally we would "double date" when John McBride dated her friend, Judy Bowman. However, I was younger than her and not very mature. I had skipped grade four and was always the youngest kid in the class. I probably preferred to spend my time catching frogs. I was also a bit like that Peanuts character Linus who buries his head in his piano and can't think of doing anything else. Mary Lou was always patient with me. We ended our romance at the end of grade nine and I didn't have a regular steady girlfriend until grade 12.

TOM WARDEN

In the Spring of 1970, when I was preparing to graduate from VMS, I noticed a kid that kept hanging around after school that was my age, but I had never seen before. It turned out to be Tom Warden, who attended the Catholic school at the time. We struck up a friendship and hung out together for a few years. A very gregarious personality, he also had an interest in music and could play the piano. His father was very involved in community politics and owned Warden's Appliances on King Street, a retail store just like the one in the movie "That Thing You Do".

During the summer of 1970, I had temporarily taken over Martin Loveridge's London Free Press paper route for a couple of weeks. This entailed getting up at around 6:00 a.m. and getting the newspapers delivered before breakfast. One night, I had Tom at my house for a sleep-over and we stayed up past midnight watching Johnny Carson's "Tonight Show". Since we were already awake, we decided that it would be neat to get the paper route completed in the middle of the night. So we quietly slipped our bikes out and met the delivery truck at 3:00 a.m. and distributed the papers to the customers, careful not to wake up the neighbourhood dogs. After the newspapers were delivered, we just rode around town with the streetlights shimmering on the rain-soaked streets until dawn. We sneaked back to my house just in time so that nobody knew we were out all night. It was the first time I had stayed up all night, but I was thankful to share this adventure with Tom.

Tom was also the only person I knew who got his full driver's license just one week after his sixteenth birthday. He was very eager to drive. In those days, you just had to pass the beginner's written test, then drive around Ingersoll for the practical test. Driving around Ingersoll was not a challenge. Everyone knew the route the examiner took and where you would be asked to parallel park. Tom passed everything with flying colours and was out driving around by himself before I even turned sixteen! Good for Tom! These days with graduated licensing and prohibitive insurance, it is almost impossible for sixteen-year-olds to drive around on their own.

PETER COX

Around the time that I met Tom Warden, he introduced me to a classmate of his, Peter Cox. Even at a young age, Pete was well-know to have a superior technical mind. He was someone who could take a lawn mower engine or television apart and put it back together. He was also a fine musician who specialised on bass instruments. Piano players and guitar players are always looking to find bass players because talented ones are very rare. Pete proved to be a wonderful, creative musician on the bass and showed me the advantages of having a "fretless" bass. For the next ten years during my association with the folk group, Peter was a great friend and musician. He was an important part of my wedding in 1979 and I bought my first television set from him.

MIKE BANNON

On the first day of high school, Mr. Riddolls briefly presented all the musical wind instruments available to students to play in class, then asked us to be ready to choose which one we would like to learn the next day. Being keen about music, I went back to the music room after school to find out more about the instruments and make a decision. When I entered the back room where all the instruments were kept, there was Mike. He was a student I had never met before because he went to the Catholic elementary school. He was also very keen about music.

Together we discussed what instrument we might play. We instinctively knew it was an important decision because we might be stuck with the instrument for the next few years. We didn't pick the flute, because only girls played flute. Clarinet was also a girly instrument and not found in any rock band. Drums were very popular, but Mr. Riddolls wasn't going to have any percussionist in first year. Only fat boys played tuba. The french horn looked like this strange instrument where you stuck your hand in and played a lot of wrong notes. Nobody could hear the french horn anyway with your hand in it. Many classmates were very eager to play the two most popular instruments; trumpet and saxophone. However, Mike and I were leaning towards something a bit more unusual, something that presented more of a challenge. We decided on a brass instrument that had a simple design with no valves. It was the slide trombone.

At the time, when rock groups were wildly popular, the ticket to fame and fortune was to play an instrument that was featured in rock bands. Two very prominent bands that had branched out from guitars and featured wind instruments were *Chicago* and *Blood, Sweat, and Tears*. Both of those bands included trombone players. Therefore, it was settled, from this point on Mike and I would both learn to play the trombone.

This proved to be a momentous decision. For the next five years of high school, Mike and I would sit together in orchestra, band, pit orchestra, quintet and marching band playing our trombones. We would both eventually purchase trombones. We both auditioned for the Faculty of Music admissions on trombone and spent our first year of university rooming together. I would often have the trombone on my lips for over two hours a day in the final years of university and eventually play in four municipal bands for thirty years on trombone. All of that trombone insanity can be traced to that first day of high school where I met Mike and we made a choice about a musical instrument.

Caption: Me and My Trombone in Grade 13

After making friends in music class, I noticed that Mike and I had many of the same classes together in grade 9; Geography, French, Art, Science, and Phys. Ed. Before semestered classes became common, you went to all eight classes in one day. You had five minutes to get to the 35 minute class, so many of my memories of grade nine are walking with Mike to our next classroom.

A few months later, Mike invited me to join a "folk" group that was going to perform at his church. He was an excellent guitar player, and I played my recently acquired upright portable organ. Ed Wrona was the other guitarist and Peter Cox rounded up the instrumentalists on bass. I was introduced to his two older sisters, Kathy and Judy, as well as the two Van Pol sisters; Yvonne and Maria who were the main vocalists. After these older girls graduated, the group was very fortunate to have Mary Ann Vlemmix take over as lead vocalist. She had the strongest and best voice of them all and by the final years of the folk group, we didn't have any other lead vocalist than Mary Ann.

Meeting Mike was a great way to grow as a musician. We would look at the music and ponder chord symbols such as F#9(#11)/E and work out the theory until we played the correct chord. We also became creative and added vocal harmony to the group. I often figured out and sang a bass part that fit the root chords with passing notes, while Mike created a corresponding tenor part. We applied it to such tunes as the "Wedding Song" and often had three or even four part harmony which sounded really neat!

Another musical adventure Mike and I had the pleasure of experiencing was the "School of Rock" group led by Bruce Flemming. Bruce was a professional keyboard musician who had been on the musical travel circuit with rock groups such as "Sound Spectrum" and "Truck". He had returned home to Ingersoll when employment as a musician was scarce and decided to give back to the community. In 1972, he rounded up all the interested high-school musicians and formed a super rock group of about 18 musicians. We often met in his basement to work on the hand-written parts in brass sectionals. Mike Bannon and I were proud to play the trombone parts to great Chicago and Joe Cocker hits. I was grateful to also get on stage and play a couple of Elton John songs on piano for our one and only concert at the Ingersoll Arena. This was a wonderful experience for Mike and I as it stimulated our desire to pursue careers in music.

Nobody could make me laugh as much as Mike could. He was a talented artist who could render a brilliant cartoon caricature of teachers and professors that was hilarious. Once we held an imaginary flatulence contest where various teachers were pretending to pass wind and get a high score for their efforts. He pretended to be Granny Ackert. His facial contortions and reactions to her labours in producing sufficient flatulence made me laugh so hard I was literally rolling around on the floor gasping for breath and grabbing my sore ribs. Such a wonderful sense of humour that I will never forget.

WISHING YOU WERE HERE...

COUSIN'S COTTAGE

As a youngster, I travelled to a few interesting places that have left a lasting impression on me. First, I will always treasure the memories of Uncle Terry and Aunt Elsie's cottage on the shore of Lake Temiskaming. Situated right across the bay from the town of New Liskeard, the cottage offered a beautiful view of the town and nearby Hailibury. The Quebec border was just a short drive around the bend and there you would find some wonderful villages dominated by a single Catholic church. I would splash in the lake with cousins Janice, Donald, Judy and David. One of my first canoeing experiences was paddling across the bay with cousin Donald into the town. Elsie's father took us out on his small boat where I caught my first lake bass.

One particularly memorable excursion with our cousins was a trip to Moosonee on the Northland Express train. We left from the cottage in New Liskeard and travelled as far North as roads could take us to the town of Cochrane. There we boarded a train and journeyed through five hours of boreal forest to the town on the bank of James Bay. It was a lot of fun hopping through all the train cars as we made our way through the never ending woodlands. When we arrived at Moosonee, we walked across town and took a motor boat through the choppy waters of the Moose River to the town of Moose Factory. There we toured a school and a church and bought some moccasins from the First Nations people who lived there. I have never been to the Arctic, but this excursion to Northern Ontario provided a glimpse of what the far north of Canada is like.

Cousins Janice, Judy, David and Donald circa 1968 in front of the cottage

NEW YORK CITY

On March 16, 1968, Robert F. Kennedy, Senator for New York, declared his candidacy for President of the United States. On that very day, I was travelling with my family for 12 hours in our blue Ford Falcon for a March break vacation in New York City. When we arrived at our hotel, hundreds of college students were crowding the streets as a huge political rally in support of Kennedy had just ended. The hotel bellman led our family to our room on the 9th floor. The hallway of the hotel was packed with young students lining the corridors. When we got to our room, to our surprise, there was a young man and a woman lying on the bed! I think they had only been in the room for a few minutes because they both had their clothes on. The bellman scolded the kids to get out of the room as the girl sheepishly tugged at her dress and the boy grabbed his jacket. Anyway, Dad told the hotel manager that we needed a different room and they arranged for us to take a penthouse suite way up on the 54th floor. A superior upgrade at no extra cost. New York City was certainly an exciting place to visit!

I recall looking down from the lofty heights of our suite to the people below. We were so far up that they looked like tiny ants. Some of the highlights of our tour of New York included the Empire State Building, St. Patrick's Cathedral, Central Park, Wall Street and the Statue of Liberty. One thing I saw for the first time was a pay toilet. I had to go to the bathroom and Dad found this public washroom where all the stalls were locked and you had to pay 10 cents to enter. Never expected to see that! This was a time before the twin towers of 9/11 notoriety were built. After a few days of our whirlwind tours of the city we headed back to the relative tranquility of Ingersoll. Along the New York State highway we saw a long convoy of green military vehicles travelling on the other side. A full mile of green jeeps, troop transports, tanks on floats and lots of artillery heading towards New York. It was the height of the Vietnam War and all this military hardware was a part of it.

ROME

In the autumn of 1971, my Latin teacher, Mr. Derbyshire, announced that there would be a March Break trip to Rome, Italy for the incredible price of only $299! I told my mom and she paid for my brother and I to join the IDCI contingent on the 1972 tour of Italy. What a fabulous opportunity this was to see a fascinating part of Europe!

There were about 50 students and teachers from our school that took this excursion. Some of the people I remember on the trip were Mr. and Mrs. Doug Harris, Mr. and Mrs. Riddolls, Dave and Tom Warden, Tom Talbot, Dan Dunlop and Mary Lou Robotham. A whole busload of Ingersoll people travelling through the exotic countryside of Italy.

We stayed in a monastery on the outskirts of Rome. There were four boys to a barracks-like room and the washroom down the hall accommodated about 20 people. The morning meal was buns and jam - my first "continental" breakfast. Our bus driver was a jolly Italian man named Bino. He enjoyed entertaining us with soccer ball tricks while we waited for all passengers to get on board. He was an amazing driver who steered the bus through impossible twists and turns of narrow city streets.

Our extensive tour of Rome included guided explorations of the Pantheon, Colloseum, Forum and many lovely public squares and fountains. During our visit to the Vatican we marvelled at the majesty of Michelangelo's Sistine Chapel. After our Vatican tour all the Canadians on the March Break trip had a short audience with Pope Paul.

We took one side trip to the city of Pompeii. This ancient city was destroyed by a volcano nearly two thousand years ago and remained buried until recent archaeological excavations uncovered the fascinating site. I recall a man with a long black cape directing us through the ruins and explaining the treasures in a thick Italian accent. We all thought he looked like Dracula.

Another expedition brought us to the beautiful city of Florence. There we toured the Cathedral of Santa Maria del Fiore, the bronze baptistery doors, and saw the famous "David" statue in the Accademia Gallery. We also had some free time to chase the pigeons through the Palazzo Vecchio and hang out at the famous Ponte Vecchio. At the end of the tour through the Accademia, the tour guide asked if anyone had any questions. Being the smartass that I was, I asked what damage had occurred to the priceless works of art during the terrible flood of Florence 6 years earlier. I had read a National Geographic article about the horrendous flooding that occurred in 1966. The tour guide then pointed to a watermark about 4 feet off the ground that showed how high the waters had risen. Yes indeed, the flood nearly destroyed many treasures of the Renaissance.

Tom Talbot and I feeding the pigeons on the Palazzo in Florence, Italy 1972

The final stop on our grand Italian tour was Pisa, to see the leaning tower. The tower certainly was leaning at a crazy angle! In 1972, you could climb round and round the many stories and there wasn't much in the way of guard rails. A few years later, engineers sounded the alarm that the Leaning Tower of Pisa might soon crash to the ground, so extensive excavations were undertaken to anchor and stabilize the tower so future generations could enjoy the famous landmark.

The March Break tour of Italy is like a flower in my memory. I had never been to Europe, or even on a large plane before. To see so many wonders of the world and artistic treasures was an exhilarating experience that certainly stimulated my passionate interest in History. It was wonderful to share it with friends from Ingersoll.

I travelled back to Italy 30 years later and things have changed considerably. Hundreds of busloads of tourists descend upon the key sites every day leaving long lines to pass through safety measures. Back in 1972, tourists could walk into the Vatican without security personnel checking all your belongings prior to admission. Once inside, you could walk right up to the Pieta statue and even touch it. Now the priceless art works are encased in glass and tourists need to stand at a distance to observe it. The enjoyment of appreciating the treasures is very diminished everywhere in Europe. I am so glad I had the opportunity to see Italy before the wall of security went up.

ALGONQUIN PARK

In August 1973, the Ingersoll Parks and Recreation Department advertised a camping trip to Algonquin Park. For $50, young people could participate in a 4-day excursion led by Tom Talbot. We were told not to bring any tents or food as we only needed a sleeping bag and a warm sweater since everything would be taken care of. We would be sleeping "under the stars"! About 15 young Ingersoll citizens piled into a mini- van and we made our way to the park.

We rented five heavy aluminum canoes and divided up so that 3 people shared each canoe. It was nearly nightfall when we set up camp and ate boiled beans and bread.

We pulled the canoes out of the water and tilted them to cover our heads and slept on the hard ground with only the canoe for protection. This was indeed "roughing it!"

The next day, we found ourselves on a very long portage trying to carry the heavy canoes through the bush. It was very cumbersome for three people to manoeuvre the boat on dry land until one sturdy lad showed us how much faster you could go if you managed to get the canoe up on your head! Yes, we had discovered that the proper way to portage a canoe was to hoist it up on your shoulders and carry it alone.

For the next three days we hiked and paddled deep into the interior heartland of Algonquin Park. Awake at dawn and trekking until we were exhausted at dusk, we set up camp anywhere there was dry land. The leaders often stopped and huddled in the middle of the lake to decipher the map and figure out which direction to take.

We took a classic loop of Canoe Lake, Littledoe Lake, Tom Thompson Lake, McIntosh Lake, Grassy Lake, Trout Lake, Big Trout Lake, Otterslide Lake and finally Burnt Island Lake before returning to Canoe Lake. All of these beautiful lakes are connected by foot portages. No motorboats allowed! Absolute silence in the stillness of the wilderness. Stars shine brighter than anywhere else so far from civilisation. Breathtaking beauty surrounds you as if you are in the middle of a Tom Thompson painting.

This tour of Algonquin Park in 1973 was unforgettable. It left an enduring impression on my soul. I have returned to the park 10 times later in my life, mostly with brother-in-law Arnie Judge and my two sons. Packing lightly and renting a lightweight Kevlar canoe is definitely the best way to explore this wilderness. I would encourage anyone who wants to comprehend Canada's early history and vast geography take a tour of Algonquin Park in a canoe. I have told my family that when I die, I wish that my ashes be scattered over Big Trout Lake because I know I will be closer to God.

WE CAN WORK IT OUT...

VOYAGEUR RESTAURANT

It has been said that getting a difficult, boring, low-paying job when you are young may inspire you to stay in school and aspire to a better profession and career. I think that is certainly true in my case. My first summer job was a dishwasher at the large Voyageur Restaurant on Highway 401 between Ingersoll and Woodstock. Busloads of travellers would crowd into the restaurant and spoon out their Salisbury Steak or Shepherd's Pie onto plates leaving a mountain of dishes to be cleaned non-stop for eight hours. The machine that washed them was often taxed to the limit and sometimes broke down, leaving cartloads of dishes to be washed by hand. I often worked the night shift and that meant scraping out the crockery for the cook and getting caught up for the next day's deluge.

Dishwasher was the lowest job in the hierarchy of restaurant employment. Eventually I worked my way up to busboy, where I cleaned the tables and picked up all the dishes for the unlucky schmuck washing the dishes. One night when the maintenance man didn't show up, I put on this blue uniform and scrubbed the floors and cleaned the toilets. Maybe dishwasher wasn't so bad after all. The wage for all of this work was $1.65 per hour. A full days work got you slightly more than 10 dollars.

It was the dawning of the age of "fast food". Today when you stop along the highway and order some food, it is wrapped in a cardboard box and you get your drink in a cardboard cup. If you are given cutlery at all, it is plastic and you eat with your hands and throw all the packaging out when you finish eating. Back in 1973, people lined up for their cafeteria-style food with ceramic plates, steel cutlery and beverage glasses. All of these dishes were washed and recycled for the next customer. Probably a lot more labour-intensive, but a lot less garbage for landfill sites.

I really detested the job of dishwasher. The restaurant was very chaotic behind the scenes with constant turnover of untrained teenage staff. Working the night-shift, I would arrive home from work just as the sun was rising on a glorious summer day. I would sleep most of the day, then soon after supper I would catch the van to take me out to the restaurant and spend the whole night scrubbing dishes. I needed an escape. I remember doing some research on Music Camps and finding one in Beaverton, Ontario that had a few openings. I told my parents that Music Camp would be vitally important for me because I may want a career in music and with the wages I had saved I would pay for the entire experience myself. My mom didn't seem to mind at all and even encouraged me to go to camp, since we were planning to drive up to New Liskeard near the end of the summer anyway. It was a very happy day when I told the manager that I would not be coming back to the Voyager Restaurant to wash dishes.

Music camp was rather intense with a few private trombone lessons, sectionals, small ensembles and large band rehearsals. I found that I was not very good on trombone compared to the other students and many of the young musicians were serious and competitive. It was one thing to pride myself on being the second-best trombone player in all of Ingersoll but quite another to find myself surrounded by the best trombone students in all of Ontario. Anyway, I was happy just to enjoy the daylight and not be stuck in a hot room scrubbing away at dishes. I recall reading *Future Shock* by Alvin Toffler in the little free time I had. This book was a fascinating commentary on the rapid changes taking place in modern society and predicted the stress and anxiety that pervades the lives of people who yearn for a simpler time.

P. T. WALKER FURNITURE

As grade 12 began, I got a phone call from a Mr. Walker asking if I would be interested in an after-school job working at his furniture store. This was probably the largest store in the downtown area of Ingersoll. Mike Bannon was working next door at Donny Douglas furniture and had put in a good word for me as a recommendation. I would work every day except Wednesday after school for two hours, then all day Saturday. The pay was $25 / week. Duties included assembling and delivering tables, chairs, couches and all varieties of furniture. I also vacuumed the rugs and polished the furniture in the show rooms as well as washed the large glass windows in the front of the store. I particularly enjoyed going out on deliveries with Mr. Harold Robotham.

Things went very well for the first few months, until business seemed to slow down dramatically as the winter wore on. I sometimes found myself getting all caught up on my chores with nothing much to do. I noticed the three salesmen often just sitting in a circle waiting for infrequent customers. So, I decided to do the same and join them in the huddle. Mr. Walker asked me if I had all my tasks completed and I assured him that I did. I could tell from the annoyed look on his face that he wasn't happy with my answer.

When I reflect back on it now, there was a kind of ranking of positions in the store where the salesmen were more valued than the subservient chore boy and integrating with higher-paid company was a bit like Daisy mixing it up with Lady Grantham from Downton Abby. To stay employed, it's probably best to at least "look busy" even if you are not. It didn't help much that I brought a novel to read at work. It certainly didn't help when I asked the manager why anyone would want to buy this high priced furniture when they could go a few miles down the road to Woodstock or London to buy less expensive items.

ALEXANDRA HOSPITAL

I didn't get asked back to P. T. Walker Furniture the next year, so I went looking for a different part-time job in my final year of high school. My mother was a nurse at the local hospital and my brother had worked as an ambulance driver, so I enquired about the possibility of employment at the hospital. There was a part-time vacancy for a housekeeping / janitorial position and with the help of my mother, I was hired. The weekend job entailed mopping all the floors of the hospital, taking out all the garbage and making sure all public areas were clean. At $3 / hour, it was a substantial improvement in pay!

On my first few days of the job, I approached my tasks with great gusto, swinging the mop down the corridors and hurriedly taking out all the trash. To my surprise, I was capable of getting all of the required work completed in four hours, even though my shift lasted for eight hours. I told my mom about how fast I could get the jobs completed, but she advised me to keep quiet about it and slow down because it was a "unionised" position.

Everything went smoothly with the job for the next few months until we got to March. I was in my last year of high school and I was making applications to university and knew that the results from examinations written in March would be crucial in determining acceptance to university. I had also applied for the Firestone scholarship and needed an average mark over 80% in all my science and math courses to be successful. I was working on a Sunday and a critical Physics exam was scheduled for the next day. So I whipped through my chores at the hospital and went down to the empty locker room and pulled out my Physics text and notebooks and began serious study. While I was studying, I had an unexpected visitor. It was the local union boss of housekeeping who just happened to walk into the locker room on his day off and saw me sitting there surrounded by Physics notes.

On the one hand, everything went very well with the Physics exam the next day. I received the top mark of the class on the exam and eventually succeeded in earning the scholarship. However, I got a phone call from my supervisor telling me that I was fired! No judge, jury, or reprimand...just the executioner! What I learned from this experience was that if you find yourself getting a job done in half the time, you're probably doing a pretty sloppy job. If you are fortune enough to land a well-paying job you complete in a short time, keep quiet about it and thank your lucky stars! Considering that I went on to university and won some scholarships, I think that on the whole, my day spend studying for Physics was probably worth losing the custodial job but nobody would nominate me for Employee of the Week!

PARKS AND RECREATION

In the summer before university, dad arranged for me to be interviewed for a job with the Ingersoll Recreation Department providing bus transportation for handicapped kids for their various programs. I was asked if I knew how to drive a standard stick shift. "Sure," I said, "I drove the tractor all over the farm as a kid". I was lying. In reality I only had one disastrous day popping the clutch and grinding the gears on the farm tractor when I was 10 years old. The day arrived when I was to pick up the mini-bus and drive the 12 playground leaders across Southern Ontario to their destination at Bark Lake. Mike Bannon was very kind-hearted to show me the skills I needed to operate the mini-bus and in half an hour I was competent enough with the stick shift to slowly change gears and keep the motor from stalling.

The bus driver job was probably the most fun I ever had on any job. I would drive around town picking up kids and playground counsellors and take them to their various destinations. Meanwhile, the leaders were stuck in one location all summer long, while I had the great freedom to travel about town.

I particularly enjoyed driving the kids over the rough road behind Maude Wilson pool and giving them a fun bumpy ride.

Old Parks and Rec offices above Ingersoll Police station

Victoria Park

Driving Tractor for Ingersoll parks wearing inverted t-shirt

This photo appeared in London Free Press due to my unusual headgear

Monday May 3, 1976 was a snowy day. I know this because this was my first day on the Parks maintenance job cutting lawns in all of Ingersoll's parks. I was delivered to Lion's Park with a hand mower and started to cut the lawn in the bitter cold. Soon after I started, snow flurries descended in a blizzard of white making it rather difficult to continue. Eventually, the supervisor, Wally Smith, drove around to pick me up as he decided it was rather futile to cut grass in a snowstorm.

The lawn maintenance job was a great way to stay in shape. The skills I learned in driving the bus came in handy when I drove the tractor mower. It was exciting driving the tractor through town as traffic piled up behind me. The lawn cutting job only lasted a couple months until the really enjoyable job of bus driver started up again in July.

THE INGERSOLL TIMES

My first day on the job required me to quickly learn to operate a camera. So I went down to the little park at the corner of Charles and King and snapped a few pictures. On the steps of the small pavilion was a skinny old man lying down. The old man was "Dutch" Savage, the homeless town drunk. I took a few pictures of him and returned to develop the pictures. Later that day after work, I drove past the park and noticed him still lying down in the same position. Around midnight, the town police observed him and brought him out of the cold to the jail cell where he could spend the night. Sometime that night he died in the jail cell of alcohol poisoning and hypothermia.

Whenever someone dies in police custody, there is a full judicial inquest into the circumstances regarding someone's death. The inquest was held in the counsel chambers of the town hall. I was called to testify before Judge Groom that I took the pictures and observed Dutch Savage's last day alive.

Last hours of Dutch Savage

This photo was used at police inquest and shows exposure testing techniques of old photography.

This is just one of the many interesting stories that I was part of as a roving reporter for the local newspaper, The Ingersoll Times. My dad was the sportswriter for the paper, and he helped me secure the position. In the summers of 1978 and 1979, I became the town journalist. Sometimes I was a columnist expressing my opinion on a variety of local topics, sometimes I wrote feature articles and most of the time I just followed the news of whatever was happening in the town. Some of the highlights included riding around town in a police cruiser for the night and writing about the adventure. In reality, the only "action" was catching three young men walking along the sidewalk with beer bottles and the officer writing out a citation for breaking the law. Ingersoll that night was a pretty safe town.

In the days before the internet, people actually read newspapers. I conducted many interviews for the Times. One of them was with my grandpa, Fred Smith, about his participation in World War I. Another time I interviewed Terry Bannon, Mike's brother, about his evacuation from Iran when the Ayatollah overthrew the Shah during the 1978 revolution. Perhaps the most memorable interview was with Byron Jenvies, the town historian. Byron had a column in the newspaper called "The Jenvie Files" where he recounted his own personal stories of when he was young. Byron Jenvies was born in 1880. When I interviewed him he was 99 years old and had no signs of dementia. He lived alone on a house on Ann Street and invited me in to his home for the interview. He remembered the time when Sir John A. MacDonald, Canada's first Prime Minister, was our leader. He remembered when most of the roads in the region were just horse trails hacked through the wilderness. It was really exhilarating for me to make a personal connection to the distant past and motivated my desire to take Canadian History courses at university.

Photography has made incredible progress in the past decade. Today you can snap a picture on a smart phone and instantly share it with anyone around the world. Back in the seventies, it was a laborious process. First, you loaded a roll of film onto your camera and you were limited to just 24 pictures. When you finished taking snapshots, you had to develop the roll by carefully placing it into a metal canister filled with chemicals. In the darkroom with only low red light to see what you were doing, you filled some small pans with chemicals and immersed the special photo paper into them until the desired image slowly appeared. I was glad to be trained in the art of photography because they were needed for newspaper articles that I wrote and it was a relatively expensive and time consuming process.

AND IN THE END...

The job of newspaper journalist ended on August 22, 1979. Three days later I was married to Sherry and moved to London for a year of teacher's college. I would return only on weekends for the church organist job. Then came the fateful day in April 1980 when I accepted employment in Kitchener. It was the end of picturing myself settling into the town of Ingersoll for the rest of my life. I had come to know many town citizens through my job as a reporter. I had criss-crossed the town for many years sometimes in a tractor and sometimes in a mini-bus through my employment with Parks and Recreation. All of my high school days and many years of public school were in Ingersoll.

Today there is no Ingersoll Times. There is no P. T. Walker Furniture - just a large gazebo in the middle of town. The old police station and recreation offices are gone. Victory Memorial School is now empty. Downtown businesses seem to be struggling to survive. The town is dominated by a large auto assembly plant where workers arrive and leave without ever seeing the main street. However, I resist the urge to lament the inevitable changes as Ingersoll continues to evolve like all other communities. For instance, Maude Wilson pool was replaced by a lovely indoor swimming pool located in Victoria Park right where I parked the tractor used to cut the grass in Ingersoll parks.

Ingersoll was what I might call a "Goldilocks" town. Not too big, not too small, but just right in size. Small towns that I was familiar with like Salford, Thamesford, and Dutton seemed to me too diminutive to offer much in the way of cultural simulation. On the other hand, I have lived in the sprawling monotonous suburbs of a large city where you just don't feel a sense of community. Ingersoll had a distinctive cooperative spirit and identity. It was small enough that you could bike anywhere to a friend's house or be out in the country in a matter of minutes. When I grew up there, it seemed to have everything I needed.

Looking back, I find churches and religion to be a strong influence. My father studied one year at seminary. I married a preacher's daughter. My best friend in high school became a pastor. Churches were an anchor through my various roles as Sunday School student, Cub Scout, altar boy, choir boy, folk singer and organist. All of the denominations of religion in Ingersoll welcomed me with open arms. It is disheartening to see so many churches struggle through this era of decline with nothing much to replace them.

Best of all, it was the people of Ingersoll that gave me such a great start in life. My family offered unconditional love and support with a large measure of freedom. Driving me out to music lessons year after year without questioning my commitment to practicing. People like Stuart Little, Aunt Mildred and Byron Jenvie kindled my passion for History. People like Bruce Fleming inspired our dreams of rock n' roll glory. Great boyhood friends shared many childhood adventures. My wonderful friend and mentor Harold Riddolls inspired me in a career choice that I really appreciated. Yes, the people of my hometown gave me so much more than I was ever able to pay back.

Some day I may come across the music to Leroy Anderson's "Forgotten Dreams" and sit down and play it on the piano. Relive the pensive melody as my thoughts meander through the days of my childhood. All of my changes were there. The dream is gone, but I will never forget my hometown, Ingersoll.

Downtown Ingersoll, 2013

Provided by author Brian J. Smith

Printed in the United States
By Bookmasters